SOR
JUANA'S

LOVE POEMS

POEMAS
DE AMOR

Sor Juana's Love Poems

Sor Juana Inés de la Cruz

Translations by
Jaime Manrique and Joan Larkin

The University of Wisconsin Press

The University of Wisconsin Press
1930 Monroe Street
Madison, Wisconsin 53711

www.wisc.edu/wisconsinpress/

3 Henrietta Street
London WC2E 8LU, England

5   4   3   2   1

Printed in the United States of America

Library of Congress Cataloging-in-Publication Data
Juana Inés de la Cruz, 1651–1695.
    Sor Juana's love poems / Sor Juana Inés de la Cruz ;
    translations by Jaime Manrique and Joan Larkin.
    p. cm.
    Originally published: New York : Painted Leaf Press,
    c1997.
    English translation with original Spanish text.
    ISBN 0-299-18704-7 (pbk. : alk. paper)
    1. Love poetry, Mexican. 2. Love poetry, Mexican—
Translations into English. I. Manrique, Jaime, 1949– II.
Larkin, Joan. III. Title.
PQ7296.J6 A24   2003
861'.3—dc21   2002075669

Woodcut of Sor Juana Inés de la Cruz. *Obras:* Madrid,
1725, courtesy of the Hispanic Society of America, New
York.
The vignettes are taken from *Viñetas Y Grabados
Ornamentales Del Siglo XVIII,* Archivo De La Nación,
México, 1980.

Acknowledgments

The translators wish to acknowledge their great debts: to Lourdes Blanco, whose knowledge of women's monastic life in Mexico in Sor Juana's day and whose generous gift to us of her time and research served as illumination and inspiration; to Gerry Gomez Pearlberg, who read these translations with care and gave valuable advice; and to our publisher, Bill Sullivan, who believed in this project and made it possible.

The publisher wishes to thank Michael Codding of the Hispanic Society of America for his invaluable help. Thanks also to Miguel Falquez-Certain, Griffin Handsbury, James Mazle, Brian Brunius, and of course, my wonderfully patient colleague, Terry Marks.

Contents

Sor Juana Inés de la Cruz

Foreword

Sor Juana and Love

The idea for this volume first came to me a few years ago when I was teaching at Mount Holyoke College a course on love and sexuality in Latin American literature. It seemed to me the logical place to start was the poetry of Sor Juana Inés de la Cruz, the Mexican nun (1648/51-1695) who is the most important writer of colonial times in Latin America, and one of the geniuses the Americas have produced.

After her death, Sor Juana was almost completely forgotten. Two hundred years went by until, in the beginning of the 20th century, her writings were rediscovered by women scholars. It is in the second half of our century that her works have become readily available to lay readers. In our time, Sor Juana (thanks in part to Octavio Paz's magisterial biographical study) has entered the canon and is widely studied as a writer and thinker.

Rescued as a feminist symbol, Sor Juana is nowadays better known for polemical works such as *The Answer*, her response to the efforts of the Mexican Church to silence her (they succeeded, and it is a miracle that so many of Sor Juana's works survived). Of her poetry, every student in a Spanish department knows the poem that begins, *Hombres necios que acusáis* (Foolish and accusing men), Sor Juana's blistering attack on male chauvinism. Taken up by feminist thinkers as a heroine, Sor Juana is better known for her tragic story and her philo-sophical and theological writings than for her poetry.

What a great poet she was! If she had writtten only *The First Dream* it would be enough to place her next to Blake and Dante—the very greatest visionaries. But it seems to me that it is in her sonnet-making that Sor Juana achieves her highest peaks. As a sonneteer, she's right there alongside Petrarch, Shakespeare, Donne, Góngora and Quevedo, the masters of the form. And it is in the sonnets about love that Sor Juana transcends the conventions of the Age of the Baroque to become an original, universal and immortal poet.

In my readings of Sor Juana's poetry, I noticed that many of her poems dwelt on the subject of love. Once I was able to isolate them, to cull them from her vast production, I saw that writing about love was for Sor Juana an expression of a deep psychic, spiritual and emotional need. Whereas a religious poet such as St. John of the Cross composed sublime love poetry about the mystical union of man, his soul and God (although a reading of the poems as homoerotic texts is also valid), Sor Juana's religious poems seem to me nothing more than accomplished exercises, as if her whole mind and soul did not go into their making. However, when she writes about love and sensuality, Sor Juana soars above her age, and becomes our true contemporary— not just because of her gender-bending and transgressive sexuality, but because her love poems are expressions of a complex and ambivalent modern psyche, and because they are so passionate and ferocious that when we read them we feel consumed by the naked intensity she achieves.

So I've selected from Sor Juana's broad production on the many shapes of love some of the poet's most arresting reflections on the subject, making as varied a selection as possible to us at this time, merely hoping to suggest the riches that lie in that direction. I wanted this little book to be a smorgasbord of her many poetic delights and to serve as a guide to readers who are interested in Sor Juana's politics as well as her supreme artistry. As a poet, she is, I think, one of the most carnal bards of all time: bawdy, tactile, fiery, elegiac, she hits multiple notes, always insisting on the importance of desire.

Sor Juana's first volume of poetry, *Inundación castálida,* was published in Spain by the Vicereine María Luisa Manrique de Lara y Gonzaga, Countess of Paredes, Marquise de la Laguna. María Luisa was also a source of inspiration for the Mexican poet, the Lysi of the love poems.

It gives me enormous pleasure to link once more the Manrique name to Sor Juana's trajectory, which becomes more dazzling and pertinent as time passes.

Jaime Manrique
New York, 1997

11

El hijo que la esclava ha concebido

When a Slave Gives Birth

A la Excma. Sra. Condesa de Paredes, Marquesa de la Laguna, enviándole estos papeles que su Excia. le pidió y que pudo recoger Sor Juana de muchas manos, en que estaban no menos divididos que escondidos, como tesoro, con otros que no cupo en el tiempo buscarlos ni copiarlos

El hijo que la esclava ha concebido,

dice el Derecho que le pertenece

al legítimo dueño que obedece

la esclava madre, de quien es nacido.

El que retorna al campo agradecido,

opimo fruto, que obediente ofrece,

es del señor, pues si fecundo crece,

se lo debe al cultivo recibido.

Así, Lysi divina, estos borrones

que hijos del alma son, partos del pecho,

será razón que a ti te restituya;

y no lo impidan sus imperfecciones,

pues vienen a ser tuyos de derecho

los conceptos de una alma que es tan tuya.

Ama y Señora mía, besa los pies de V. Excia.,
su criada
Juana Inés de la Cruz

When a slave gives birth,

the Law says

her son belongs

to his mother's master.

When a harvest overflows,

fertile land thanks

with bountiful fruits

the lord who enriched the soil.

Divine Lysi, it's only fair that these lines—

children nursed at my breast—

be given back.

Flawed as they are,

I return them to their rightful owner,

creations of a soul that belongs to you.

Divina Lysi mía

My Divine Lysi

Divina Lysi mía:
perdona si me atrevo
a llamarte así, cuando
aun de ser tuya el nombre no merezco.

Y creo, no osadía
es llamarte así, puesto
que a ti te sobran rayos,
si en mí pudiera haber atrevimientos.

Error es de la lengua,
que lo que dice imperio
del dueño, en el dominio,
parezcan posesiones en el siervo.

Mi rey, dice el vasallo;
mi cárcel, dice el preso;
y el más humilde esclavo,
sin agraviarlo, llama suyo al dueño.

Así, cuando yo mía
te llamo, no pretendo
que juzguen que eres mía,
sino sólo que yo ser tuya quiero.

My divine Lysi:
forgive me for daring
to call you mine
when I'm not worthy to be called yours.

I refuse to believe
I've stepped out of line.
If calling you mine offends you,
strike me with lightning.

The tongue is mistaken
to say, *These goods
belong to the lord of the manor.*
The serf is the real owner.

My king, says the subject.
My cell, says the prisoner.
It's no crime for the lowest slave
to call his master his.

When I say *mine*
I don't pretend
anyone thinks I own you,
only that I'm hungry to be yours.

Yo te vi; pero basta:
que a publicar incendios
basta apuntar la causa,
sin añadir la culpa del efecto.

Que mirarte tan alta,
no impide a mi denuedo;
que no hay Deidad segura
al altivo volar del pensamiento.

Y aunque otras más merezcan,
en distancia del Cielo
lo mismo dista el valle
más humilde, que el monte más soberbio.

En fin, yo de adorarte
el delito confieso;
si quieres castigarme,
este mismo castigo será premio.

I've seen you—that's all I'll say.
To expose dangerous thoughts,
all you have to do is point
to what started the fire.

You may be on a pedestal,
but you won't keep me from speaking.
Even a goddess isn't safe
from a mind that dares to soar.

Some may be worthier than others,
but low valley
and exalted peak
are the same distance from Heaven.

Yes, I confess
to the crime of adoring you.
Punish me if you like—
punishment from you would be a joy.

Pedirte, Señora, quiero

I Beg You, Señora

Pedirte, Señora, quiero
de mi silencio perdón,
si lo que ha sido atención
le hace parecer grosero.

Y no me podrás culpar
si hasta aquí mi proceder,
por ocuparse en querer,
se ha olvidado de explicar.

Que en mi amorosa pasión
no fue descuido, ni mengua,
quitar el uso a la lengua
por dárselo al corazón.

Ni de explicarme dejaba:
que, como la pasión mía
acá en el alma te vía,
acá en el alma te hablaba.

Y en esta idea notable
dichosamente vivía;
porque en mi mano tenía
el fingirte favorable.

I beg you, Señora,
please forgive me
if my silence
seems insulting.

Don't accuse me
if I'm so weak from wanting
I forgot to say
I have an explanation:

Moved by my passion—
not careless, not indifferent—
I took work from my tongue
and gave it to my heart.

And like my passion
I lacked words to tell you:
I saw you in my soul.
In my soul, I spoke to you.

I lived in illusion
and was truly happy.
I held you in my hand.
and let myself imagine.

Con traza tan peregrina
vivió mi esperanza vana;
pues te pudo hacer humana
concebiéndote divina.

¡Oh cuán loca llegué a verme
en tus dichosos amores,
que, aun fingidos, tus favores
pudieron enloquecerme!

¡Oh cómo, en tu Sol hermoso
mi ardiente afecto encendido,
por cebarse en lo lucido
olvidó lo peligroso!

Perdona, si atrevimiento
fue atreverme a tu ardor puro;
que no hay sagrado seguro
de culpas de pensamiento.

De esta manera engañaba
la loca esperanza mía,
y dentro de mí tenía
todo el bien que deseaba.

I nursed a wild scheme
and fed it to my hope.
Though I saw you as a goddess
in my dream you were human.

Oh I was insane
in the sweet belief you loved me;
when you pretended,
you drove me to madness!

Oh how I went up in flames
in your lovely Sun!
Hungry for the bait,
I forgot the danger.

Forgive me. I was wrong
to dare to want your loving.
Nothing is sacred
to a woman guilty of thinking.

And so I tricked myself,
crazy with hoping.
Inside me I had
all the sweetness I wanted.

Mas ya tu precepto grave
rompe mi silencio mudo;
que él solamente ser pudo
de mi respeto la llave.

Y aunque el amar tu belleza
es delito sin disculpa,
castígueseme la culpa
primero que la tibieza.

No quieras, pues, rigurosa,
que, estando ya declarada,
sea de veras desdichada
quien fue de burlas dichosa.

Si culpas mi desacato,
culpa también tu licencia,
que si es mala mi obediencia,
no fue justo tu mandato.

Y si es culpable mi intento,
será mi afecto precito;
porque es amarte un delito
de que nunca me arrepiento.

I now break my silence—
your strict commandment—
though silence was the key
to showing my obedience.

To say I adore you
can't be forgiven.
So punish my insolence—
I'm no tepid sinnner.

My strict mistress,
now that I've said it
you want me to be wretched.
I'd be grateful if you mocked me.

You accuse me of disobedience:
remember the license you gave me.
If I rebel against you
it's because you're a cruel mistress.

And if I'm guilty for trying,
punish me as an infidel.
If loving you is a sin
don't expect me to do penance.

Esto en mis afectos hallo,
y más, que explicar no sé;
mas tú, de lo que callé,
inferirás lo que callo.

These are my feelings—
there's no other way to say it.
You know what I'm not saying.
And you know why I'm silent.

Detente, sombra de mi bien esquivo

Don't Go,
My Darling.
I Don't Want This
to End Yet

Detente, sombra de mi bien esquivo,
imagen del hechizo que más quiero,
bella ilusión por quien alegre muero,
dulce ficción por quien penosa vivo.

Si al imán de tus gracias, atractivo,
sirve mi pecho de obediente acero,
¿para qué me enamoras lisonjero
si has de burlarme luego fugitivo?

Mas blasonar no puedes, satisfecho,
de que triunfa de mí tu tiranía:
que aunque dejas burlado el lazo estrecho

que tu forma fantástica ceñía,
poco importa burlar brazos y pecho
si te labra prisión mi fantasía.

Don't go, my darling. I don't want this to end yet.
This sweet fiction is all I have.
Hold me so I'll die happy,
thankful for your lies.

My breasts answer yours
magnet to magnet.
Why make love to me, then leave?
Why mock me?

Don't brag about your conquest—
I'm not your trophy.
Go ahead: reject these arms

that wrapped you in sumptuous silk.
Try to escape my arms, my breasts—
I'll keep you prisoner in my poem.

Esta tarde, mi bien, cuando te hablaba

This Afternoon, My Darling, I Kept Talking

Esta tarde, mi bien, cuando te hablaba,
como en tu rostro y tus acciones vía
que con palabras no te persuadía,
que el corazón me vieses deseaba;

y Amor, que mis intentos ayudaba,
venció lo que imposible parecía:
pues entre el llanto, que el dolor vertía,
el corazón deshecho destilaba.

Baste ya de rigores, mi bien, baste:
no te atormenten más celos tiranos,
ni el vil recelo tu quietud contraste

con sombras necias, con indicios vanos,
pues ya en líquido humor viste y tocaste
mi corazón deshecho entre tus manos.

This afternoon, my darling, I kept talking,
but your face, your gestures
told me my words were insincere.
I just wanted you to see my heart!

Love took my part—
it was a miracle:
I wept, wept
until my heart dissolved.

Stop this torture, darling. Stop it.
Don't be so cold. You're not a tyrant
poisoning peace with cheap suspicions—

foolish fears, dire omens.
You've seen my heart and touched it:
clear liquid spilled into your hands.

Con el dolor de la mortal herida

Love Opened a
Mortal Wound

Con el dolor de la mortal herida,
de un agravio de amor me lamentaba;
y por ver si la muerte se llegaba,
procuraba que fuese más crecida.

Toda en el mal el alma divertida,
pena por pena su dolor sumaba,
y en cada circunstancia ponderaba
que sobraban mil muertes a una vida.

Y cuando, al golpe de uno y otro tiro,
rendido el corazón daba penoso
señas de dar el último suspiro,

no sé con qué destino prodigioso
volví en mi acuerdo y dije:—¿Qué me admiro?
¿Quién en amor ha sido más dichoso?

Love opened a mortal wound.
In agony, I worked the blade
to make it deeper. Please,
I begged, let death come quick.

Wild, distracted, sick,
I counted, counted
all the ways love hurt me.
One life, I thought—a thousand deaths.

Blow after blow, my heart
couldn't survive this beating.
Then—how can I explain it?

I came to my senses. I said,
Why do I suffer? What lover
ever had so much pleasure?

¿Vesme, Alcino, que atada a la cadena... ?

Look at Me, Alcino.
See the Chain?

¿Vesme, Alcino, que atada a la cadena
de Amor, paso en sus hierros aherrojada
mísera esclavitud, desesperada
de libertad, y de consuelo ajena?

¿Ves de dolor y angustia el alma llena,
de tan fieros tormentos lastimada,
y entre las vivas llamas abrasada
juzgarse por indigna de su pena?

¿Vesme seguir sin alma un desatino
que yo misma condeno por extraño?
¿Vesme derramar sangre en el camino,

siguiendo los vestigios de un engaño?
¿Muy admirado estás? ¿Pues ves, Alcino?
Más merece la causa de mi daño.

Look at me, Alcino. See the chain?
It's iron; this is how they handle slaves.
It tightens if I try to move. Love
did this to me—it's a life sentence.

See me tortured, burned, by iron, by fire?
Living flames kiss me,
and I judge myself unworthy.
See what I am? Twisted—

even I can see it.
Look at me, spilling my blood in the street
hot on the scent of a lie.

Surprised, Alcino? Look again:
the one I'm being flayed alive for
is worth even more.

¿Qué es esto, Alcino? ¿Cómo tu cordura... ?

Have You Lost Your Mind, Alcino?

¿Qué es esto, Alcino? ¿Cómo tu cordura
se deja así vencer de un mal celoso,
haciendo con extremos de furioso
demostraciones más que de locura?

¿En qué te ofendió Celia, si se apura?
¿O por qué al Amor culpas de engañoso,
si no aseguró nunca poderoso
la eterna posesión de su hermosura?

La posesión de cosas temporales,
temporal es, Alcino, y es abuso
el querer conservarlas siempre iguales.

Con que tu error o tu ignorancia acuso,
pues Fortuna y Amor, de cosas tales
la propiedad no han dado, si no el uso.

Have you lost your mind, Alcino?
Your rage frightens me;
you're becoming a monster.
Leave Celia alone—

she doesn't want you. Why
curse her? Why call it betrayal?
Did you think you could keep her?
Things change, Alcino.

Do you think you own her body?
Your lust is out of control,
abusive. I say it's you

who's guilty, ignorant. Listen:
With luck, love lends us beauty—
not the right to keep it.

Inés, yo con tu amor me *refocilo*

Inez, I Have to Gloat:
You're Gorgeous

Inés, yo con tu amor me *refocilo,*
y viéndome querer me *regodeo;*
en mirar tu hermosura me *recreo,*
y cuando estás celosa me *reguilo.*

Si a otro miras, de celos me *aniquilo,*
y tiemblo de tu gracia y tu *meneo;*
porque sé, Inés, que tú con un *voleo*
no dejarás humor ni aun para *quilo.*

Cuando estás enojada no *resuello,*
cuando me das picones me *refino,*
cuando sales de casa no *reposo;*

y espero, Inés, que entre esto y entre *aquéllo,*
tu amor, acompañado de mi *vino,*
dé conmigo en la cama o en el *coso.*

Inez, I have to gloat: you're gorgeous
and you love me. All this
pleasure—I'll never be the same.
When you're jealous, I'm a trembling thread,

and when you flirt in front of me, I die.
You flaunt those hips to drive me wild.
One thrust, you're squandering the honey
that makes me high—save it for me, Inez.

When you cover me with kisses, I'm transformed.
When you're angry with me, I can't breathe.
When you go out, I lie awake all night.

Still, Inez, none of this really matters.
Just take me to bed, where I like it,
with my wineskin and your succulent worm.

Inés, cuando te riñen por *bellaca*

Inez, When Someone Tells You You're a Bitch

Inés, cuando te riñen po *bellaca,*
para disculpas no te falta *achaque*
porque dices que traque y que *barraque;*
con que sabes muy bien tapar la *caca.*

Si coges la parola, no hay *urraca*
que así la gorja de mal año *saque;*
y con tronidos, más que un *triquitraque,*
a todo el mundo aturdes cual *matraca.*

Ese bullicio todo lo *trabuca,*
ese embeleso todo lo *embeleca;*
mas aunque eres, Inés, tan mala *cuca,*

sabe mi amor muy bien lo que se *peca:*
y así con tu afición no se *embabuca,*
aunque eres zancarrón y yo de *Meca.*

Inez, when someone tells you you're a bitch,
you've got a million comebacks. I'm supposed to think
you're some old woman full of aches and creaks—
that's your genius, dear: you cover your shit.

You have a dirty mouth; you love to use it:
once you start, no magpie can compete.
You're louder than a string of firecrackers.
You thrive on noise, you love to make a stink.

You crank out lies until a girl can't think.
Your charms are much exaggerated. Still, Inez,
the problem isn't you, you cruel pussy.

The way I love you is a sin, I know it—
but the way you fuck me is no trick. Your hard-on's real
and I'm a field just waiting to be plowed.

¿Qué pasión, Porcia, qué dolor tan ciego... ?

Portia,
What Passion,
What Blind Pain

¿Qué pasión, Porcia, qué dolor tan ciego
te obliga a ser de ti fiera homicida?
¿O en qué ofende tu inocente vida,
que así le das batalla, a sangre y fuego?

Si la Fortuna airada al justo ruego
de tu esposo se muestra endurecida,
bástale el mal de ver su acción perdida:
no acabes, con tu vida, su sosiego.

Deja las brasas, Porcia, que mortales
impaciente tu amor elegir quiere:
no al fuego de tu amor el fuego iguales;

porque si bien de tu pasión se infiere,
mal morirá a las brasas materiales
quien a las llamas del amor no muere.

Portia, what passion, what blind pain
changes you into a murdering beast?
Does your innocent life so offend you
that you scourge it with blood and fire?

Enough evil—Fortune is furious,
deaf to your husband's pleas.
Don't make him suffer your death:
leave him in peace.

Portia, your love's too brash.
Leave those lethal coals alone:
your love's not equal to those flames.

Your passion teaches us
that she who flings herself on the pyre
will never learn that love can burn you alive.

En la vida que siempre tuya fue

Divine Laura, My Life Was Always Yours

En la vida que siempre tuya fue,
Laura divina, y siempre lo será,
la Parca fiera, que en seguirme da,
quiso asentar por triunfo el mortal pie.

Yo de su atrevimiento me admiré:
que si debajo de su imperio está,
tener poder no puede en ella ya,
pues del suyo contigo me libré.

Para cortar el hilo que no hiló,
la tijera mortal abierta vi.
¡Ay, Parca fiera!, dije entonces yo;

mira que sola Laura manda aquí.
Ella, corrida, al punto se apartó,
y dejóme morir sólo por ti.

Divine Laura, my life was always yours
and always will be yours
though Death stalked me and longed
to put her foot on me and crow.

I applaud her audacity:
she's lost an empire;
now her power's yours.
Through you, I'm free.

I saw her fatal scissors
ready to snip my thread.
"Ay, Death!" I said.

"Look! Laura rules here."
Death saw she'd lost me and fled—
from now on, I die only for you.

Elegía

Elegy

En *la muerte de la Excelentísima Señora Marquesa de Mancera*

I

De la beldad de Laura enamorados
los Cielos, la robaron a su altura,
porque no era decente a su luz pura
ilustrar estos valles desdichados;

o porque los mortales, engañados
de su cuerpo en la hermosa arquitectura,
admirados de ver tanta hermosura
no se juzgasen bienaventurados.

Nació donde el Oriente el rojo velo
corre al nacer al Astro rubicundo,
y murió donde, con ardiente anhelo,

da sepulcro a su luz el mar profundo:
que fue preciso a su divino vuelo
que diese como el Sol la vuelta al mundo.

On the Death of the Most Excellent Señora the Marquise of Mancera

I

Drunk with Laura's beauty,
the sky stole her.
Her light was never meant
to blazon this wretched valley.

We the living marveled
at the perfect architecture of her body—
blind, ungrateful,
we deserved to lose her.

She rose in the East, where red curtains
rise as the Star appears in rubies;
she died where the ocean, flushed with desire,

buries Light in its deepest places.
Her brief life completed the sky;
now she's left us in darkness.

II

Bello compuesto en Laura dividido,
alma inmortal, espíritu glorioso,
¿por qué dejaste cuerpo tan hermoso
y para qué tal alma has despedido?

Pero ya ha penetrado mi sentido
que sufres el divorcio riguroso,
porque el día final puedas gozoso
volver a ser eternamente unido.

Alza tú, alma dichosa, el presto vuelo
y, de tu hermosa cárcel desatada,
dejando vuelto su arrebol en hielo,

sube a ser de luceros coronada:
que bien es necesario todo el Cielo
para que no eches menos tu morada.

II

Laura, split in two beautiful halves:
Immortal soul, glad spirit,
why tear yourself from such lovely flesh?
Why banish such a soul?

Now it dawns on me
you're suffering this cruel divorce
for the joy of meeting again
on the last day, married for all time.

Leave us, Soul. May bliss of quick flight
free you from your plush prison—
burning turned to ice.

Rise for your crown of lights:
it will take every last star
to forget this earth, your home.

III

Mueran contigo, Laura, pues moriste,
los afectos que en vano te desean,
los ojos a quien privas de que vean
hermosa luz que un tiempo concediste.

Muera mi lira infausta en que influíste
ecos, que lamentables te vocean,
y hasta estos rasgos mal formados sean
lágrimas negras de mi pluma triste.

Muévase a compasión la misma Muerte
que, precisa, no pudo perdonarte;
y lamente el Amor su amarga suerte,

pues si antes, ambicioso de gozarte,
deseó tener ojos para verte,
ya le sirvieran sólo de llorarte.

III

Laura, desire dies with you
never to be slaked. My eyes die,
stripped of the sight of you
and the light you lent them.

My unlucky lyre dies
naming you, who made me a singer.
These crude jottings
are my pen's blood tears.

Death herself will regret
her rigor, refusing to exempt you.
Love laments her bitter luck:

Once I wanted only to enjoy you,
wanted eyes only to see you.
Now I use them for weeping.

Afterword

Translating Sor Juana

The ideas and conventions Sor Juana was at home with are foreign to our time and place. She lived in a profoundly hierarchical world. Images of relationships based on the roles of servant and master, serf and feudal lord, were not merely metaphors to her. Writing about love, she often speaks of disobedience, risk, rebellion; her mastery of poetic forms offers structures for the unpardonable. She wrote in the shadow of the Inquisition, when accused heretics were tortured, sometimes burned at the stake— something she herself may have witnessed. Her experience included both viceregal court and women's monastery, privilege and restraint, patronage and repression—a life offering intellectual and creative freedom rare for a woman of her time, yet severely limiting and ultimately silencing her.

How to convey an idiom, a sensibility, a culture so different from our own? Sor Juana doesn't deserve for essential elements of her astonishing art to be lost in translation, especially now that more of her poetry is finally being published in English. But translation—especially of poetry, which is an instrument for making many choices simultaneously—always involves compromise.

With Jaime Manrique's knowledge of Spanish and mine of English, we began work on each poem by creating a word-for-word literal translation, from which I then attempted an English version we continued to work on, separately and together. Our first task was always to try to hear what lay under pressure at a depth, to try to understand Sor Juana's intentions, sometimes encoded in a formal convention or deliberately ambiguous word choice.

How literal should we be? In a word-for-word equivalent, not only underlying meanings, but the movement and surprise in the flow of Sor Juana's sounds would have disappeared, the poetry lost. We wanted to suggest her musicality. But the melting, sensual music of Sor Juana's Spanish is at one end of a continuum, the sounds of current poetry in English at the other. It felt at times as if we were taking a liquid, expansive substance and making it into something compressed, understated, harsh.

Sor Juana moves easily within the restraints of song form and sonnet, playing both with and against each form's requirements, suggesting the flow of a voice speaking with clarity and emotional force. We often found ourselves stepping into the dramatic situations she so vividly evokes. It was clear that, whether she had direct physical experience of the erotic life she wrote of, or simply observed and imagined, she was addressing living human beings who moved her. As translators, how could we show that? What would we have to give up to do it? If we faithfully reproduced her meter and rhyme, we would have to sacrifice the contemporary-sounding voice we hoped to suggest. Sor Juana's voice was often earthy, always intense, active, passionate. It sounded fresh and current to her peers—not archaic. We wanted above all to make these translations speakable, while keeping as close as possible to the tone and the emotional journey of the original.

Sor Juana had access to elegance and coarseness, high and low speech, and used the full range available to her with delicacy and wit. She played literary games (the bawdy sonnets to "Inés" are an example) in which she took words that had been given to her and wrote fourteen lines, each ending in one of the assigned words—which were a mixture of the archaic, the unusual, the comical, and the scatalogical.

There were places where we translated more freely, in the hope of achieving greater accuracy of connotation or mood. We asked ourselves how, for example, we could translate *coso* (literally "thing"), the last word in one of the sonnets to "Inés" (for whom, we noticed, Sor Juana used one of her own names). What exactly was this erotic "thing"? We first tried the perhaps too delicate, perhaps too explicit "little hand." Then, scholar Lourdes Blanco unearthed the juicy information that in Sor Juana's time, *coso* was the name for a delicacy served with liquid refreshment: a small, crisply-fried worm. Hence our translation, "your succulent worm." We trust that *coso* was as vivid an erotic reference for some of Sor Juana's contemporaries as is "succulent worm" for us, though the double-entendre is lost in an age when few of us enjoy worms as hors d'oeuvres.

When Jaime Manrique invited me to join

him on this journey, I knew that it would be full
of both challenge and pleasure, but didn't sus-
pect how dazzlingly and seductively Sor Juana's
voice would speak to me across three centuries.
I hope that her powerful character and some-
thing of what makes her poetry memorable
comes through these pages.

—Joan Larkin
New York 1997

About the Translators:

JOAN LARKIN's poetry collections are *Housework, A Long Sound,* and *Cold River.* Twice winner of the Lambda Literary award for poetry, she co-founded the independent press Out&Out Books as part of the feminist literary explosion of the 1970s and co-edited the groundbreaking anthologies *Amazon Poetry* and *Lesbian Poetry* (with Elly Bulkin) and *Gay and Lesbian Poetry in Our Time* (with Carl Morse). Her anthology of coming-out stories, *A Woman Like That,* was nominated for Publishing Triangle and Lambda awards for nonfiction in 2000.

Her writing includes *The Hole in the Sheet,* a klezmer musical farce, and two books of daily meditations in the Hazelden recovery series: *If You Want What We Have* and *Glad Day. The Living,* her verse play about AIDS, has been produced at festivals in Boston and New York. Her awards include fellowships in poetry and playwriting from the NEA, NYFA, and the Massachusetts Cultural Council. She has taught for more than three decades in MFA and college undergraduate programs and currently teaches poetry writing at Sarah Lawrence and New England College.

JAIME MANRIQUE was born in Colombia. He is the author of the novels *Colombian Gold, Latin Moon in Manhattan,* and *Twilight at the Equator.* His first book of poems received his country's National Book Award. He's the author of many books in Spanish. Among his books in English are the volumes of poems *My Night with Federico García Lorca; Tarzan, My Body, Christopher Columbus; Sor Juana's Love Poems,* co-translated with Joan Larkin; and the memoir *Eminent Maricones: Arenas, Lorca, Puig, and Me.* He has received grants from the Foundation for Contemporary Performance Arts, the New York Foundation for the Arts, and a John Simon Guggenheim Fellowship. Mr. Manrique is an associate professor in the MFA program at Columbia University.